KNOWING
GOD

JOURNAL

J. I. PACKER

WITH CAROLYN NYSTROM

InterVarsity Press
Downers Grove, Illinois

InterVarsity Press
P.O. Box 1400, Downers Grove, IL 60515
World Wide Web: www.ivpress.com
E-mail: mail@ivpress.com

InterVarsity Press® is the book-publishing division of InterVarsity Christian Fellowship/USA®, a student movement active on campus at hundreds of universities, colleges and schools of nursing in the United States of America, and a member movement of the International Fellowship of Evangelical Students. For information about local and regional activities, write Public Relations Dept., InterVarsity Christian Fellowship/USA, 6400 Schroeder Rd., P.O. Box 7895, Madison, WI 53707-7895.

The lamp, praying hands, book, clouds and pen icons used throughout the book: Roberta Polfus

Cover photograph: David Muench

ISBN 0-8308-1185-0

Printed in the United States of America ∞

19	18	17	16	15	14	13	12	11	10	9	8	7	6	5	4	3	2	1
15	14	13	12	11	10	09	08	07	06	05	04	03	02	01	00			

CONTENTS

Getting the Most Out of the *Knowing God Journal*

Stand at the crossroads and look; ask for the ancient paths, ask where the good way is, and walk in it, and you will find rest for your souls. (Jer 6:16)

On the pages of this journal is an invitation to walk the ancient paths to God. As you journey toward God, you will find nourishment and inspiration. You will deepen your knowledge of the one true God as you experience God more deeply and fully.

Each chapter of this book serves as a companion to *Knowing God*. Reading the chapters of that book along with these exercises will deepen your understanding. If you are new to journaling, you will find that this journal gives you guidance in practicing this discipline. If you are familiar with journaling, you may enjoy finding some new approaches to a favorite spiritual tool.

Each chapter helps you journal in several different ways.

 READ
■ *An Excerpt from* Knowing God.

Each chapter begins with a quote from *Knowing God* and some questions to help you start thinking about key themes from that chapter in the book.

 STUDY
■ *Knowing the God of Scripture.*

An opportunity to dig into a key Bible passage from the chapter using inductive study questions.

REFLECT
■ *Understanding the Character of God.*
This section is designed to help you focus on the aspect of the character of God that is covered in the corresponding book chapter.

 PRAY
■ *Meeting God.*
Here you will find suggestions for prayer, with a place to write out your prayers.

 JOURNAL
■ *Responding to God.*
Space to reflect on who God is and what you are learning about him.

Feel free to move through the different sections of each chapter in any order you find appealing. Most likely you will want to complete one exercise at a time. (The icons mark new exercises.) You may, however, prefer to spend a half-day in study and prayer, going through one chapter along with the book. Allow this guide to serve you in the way that best suits you.

After you complete each chapter, you may want to talk with a friend or a small group about what you are learning. There are discussion questions at the back of *Knowing God: Twentieth Anniversary Edition* that draw out the key principles of each chapter. Additionally, *Meeting God* by J. I. Packer in the LifeGuide Bible Study Series provides Bible studies on similar themes. These studies are great for a group as well as for individuals.

Not everything in this journal is planned. Fill it with prayers or thoughts from your daily life or your own favorite quotes and songs. This book is meant to encourage and inspire you, so use it as you wish.

1

THE STUDY OF GOD

READ
■ **An Excerpt from *Knowing God***

■ *Before we start to ascend our mountain of knowing God, we need to stop and ask ourselves a fundamental question. The question concerns our own motives and intentions as students: What is my ultimate aim and objective in occupying my mind with these things? What do I intend to do with my knowledge about God, once I have it?*

Note your reflection on these questions in the space below.

■ *Warning: If we pursue theological knowledge for its own sake, it is bound to go bad on us. It will make us proud and conceited. The very greatness of the subject matter will intoxicate us, and we shall come to think of ourselves as a cut above other Christians. As Paul told the conceited Corinthians, "Knowledge puffs up. . . . The man who thinks he knows something does not yet know as he ought to know" (1 Cor 8:1-2).*

STUDY
■ **Knowing the God of Scripture**

■ *Do not all children of God long to know just as much about our heavenly Father as we can learn? Yes, of course. But if you look at Psalm 119, you will see that the psalmist's concern to get knowledge about God was not a theoretical but a practical concern.*

What is one situation where what you knew about God and what you did (or felt) seemed to conflict?

Read Psalm 119:1-16. What do you sense of the author's emotional involvement in knowing God?

Mark or record all of the action words in this passage. What does the author hope to do with his knowledge of God?

List four or five of these intentions that you would like to make your own. How can you begin that process?

REFLECT
■ **Understanding the Character of God**

■ *Five basic truths about God will determine our course throughout this study:*
1. God has spoken to us, and the Bible is his Word, given to us to make us wise unto salvation.

2. God is Lord and King over his world; he rules all things for his own glory, displaying his perfections in all that he does, in order that we may worship and adore him.

3. God is Savior, active in sovereign love through the Lord Jesus Christ to rescue believers from the guilt and power of sin, to adopt them as his children and to bless them accordingly.

4. God is triune; there are within the Godhead three persons, the Father, the Son and the Holy Spirit; and the work of salvation is one in which all three act together, the Father purposing redemption, the Son securing it and the Spirit applying it.

5. Godliness means responding to God's revelation in trust and obedience, faith and worship, prayer and praise, submission and service. Life must be seen and lived in the light of God's Word. This, and nothing else, is true religion.

Reflect on these five principles of the Christian view of God. In what ways are they different from the view of God expressed by your acquaintances, the media or perhaps even your own church?

What area mentioned above would you like to make more your own as you deepen your knowledge of God?

PRAY
■ Meeting God

Meditation *before* God leads to prayer and praise *to* God. As he is the subject of our study, and our helper in it, so he must himself be the end of it. We must seek, in studying God, to be led to God. It was for this purpose that revelation was given, and it is to this use that we must put it.

Pray, using the space below to record your written response *to* God. If you need ideas for your prayer, consider looking again at Psalm 119:1-16.

■ *God, help us to put our knowledge about you to use, that we may in truth "know the Lord."*

JOURNAL
■ Responding to God

■ *The fourth question in the Westminster Shorter Catechism asks, "What is God?"*

Answer: "God is a Spirit, infinite, eternal and unchangeable in his being, wisdom, power, holiness, justice, goodness and truth."

How can we turn our knowledge about God into knowledge of God? The rule for doing this is simple but demanding. It is that we turn each truth that we learn about God into meditation before God. Meditation is the activity of calling to mind, and thinking over and dwelling on, and applying to oneself, the various things that one knows about the works, ways, purposes and promises of God. It is an activity of holy thought, consciously performed in the presence of God, under the eye of God, by the help of God and as a means of communion with God.

Using this concept of meditation, meditate on the Westminster definition of God. Consciously in God's presence record your thoughts below.

2

THE PEOPLE WHO KNOW THEIR GOD

READ
■ An Excerpt from *Knowing God*

■ *We need frankly to face ourselves. If asked how one may know God, we can at once produce the right formula: that we come to know God through Jesus Christ the Lord, in virtue of his cross and mediation, on the basis of his word of promise, by the power of the Holy Spirit, via a personal exercise of faith. Yet the gaiety, goodness and unfetteredness of spirit that are the marks of those who have known God are rare among us.*

How accurately does the description above fit you? Write your observations.

Write the name of one Christian you know who seems to possess "gaiety, goodness and unfetteredness of spirit."

How can you benefit from that person's "knowledge" of God?

STUDY
■ **Knowing the God of Scripture**

What do you see as the difference between pursuing happiness and pursuing joy?

Paul had little reason to feel happy. He was in prison; he knew he could be executed at any moment. In fact he said, "I have lost all things." Read Philippians 3:1-11. In view of this section of Paul's letter to the church at Philippi, what does it mean to "rejoice in the Lord" (v. 1)?

What reasons did Paul have at one point to think that he had known God in all the right ways (vv. 2-6)?

How is the type of "knowing God" that he describes in verses 7-11 different from the knowledge described in the previous section?

How might this section of Paul's letter help you pursue Christian joy—even in the face of personal suffering?

REFLECT
■ Understanding the Character of God

What effects does knowledge of God have on a person?

Reflect on each of the descriptions below. After each description, make notes of ways God has revealed himself in this way in your life. Note also any goals you would like to set for yourself in each area.

☐ Those who know God have great energy for God.

☐ Those who know God have great thoughts of God.

☐ Those who know God show great boldness for God.

☐ Those who know God have great contentment in God.

PRAY
■ Meeting God

■ *People who know their God are before anything else people who pray. The more knowledge, the more energy for prayer! Perhaps we are not in a position to make public gestures against ungodliness and apostasy. Perhaps we are old, or ill, or otherwise limited by our physical situation. But we can all pray about the ungodliness and apostasy we see in everyday life all around us.*

Make a list of ways you see "ungodliness and apostasy" around you—perhaps even in yourself. Then in prayer talk to God about each item on your list. Bring it to him for the work of his great and righteous power.

JOURNAL
■ **Responding to God**

The apostle Paul wrote, "I want to know Christ and the power of his resurrection and the fellowship of sharing in his sufferings" (Phil 3:10). Paul knew that knowing Christ could produce joy, even during suffering. Spend five or ten minutes meditating on this fragment from his letter. Ask God to open your heart to its meaning. Then write some of your insights, hopes and personal resolutions.

3

KNOWING AND
BEING KNOWN

READ
■ An Excerpt from *Knowing God*

■ *The world today is full of sufferers from the wasting disease which Albert Camus focused as absurdism ("life is a bad joke"), and from the complaint which we may call Marie Antoinette's fever, since she found the phrase that describes it ("nothing tastes"). These disorders blight the whole of life: everything becomes at once a problem and a bore, because nothing seems worthwhile.*

Describe an event or a stage in your life when you wondered if maybe life was a "bad joke" or when you felt as if "nothing tastes."

"This is what the LORD says: 'Let not the wise man boast of his wisdom or the strong man boast of his strength or the rich man boast of his riches, but let him who boasts boast about this: that he understands and knows me'" (Jer 9:23-24).

STUDY
■ Knowing the God of Scripture

■ *Part of the biblical concept of knowing God is that we know God only through knowing Jesus Christ, who is himself God manifest in the flesh. Jesus' voice is "heard" when Jesus' claim is acknowledged, his promise trusted and his call answered. From then on, Jesus is known as shepherd, and those who trust him he knows as his own sheep. To know Jesus is to be saved by Jesus, here and hereafter, from sin, guilt and death.*

Read John 10:27-30. What do you enjoy about this passage?

What can you know from this passage about the relationship between the shepherd (Jesus) and his sheep?

Why might a person want to be known by this shepherd?

Knowing God is work, but it is not a one-sided effort. What encouragement do you find here for your continued faith?

Reflect
■ Understanding the Character of God

■ *What does the activity of knowing God involve? First, listening to God's Word and receiving it as the Holy Spirit interprets it in application to oneself; second, noting God's nature and character as his Word and works reveal it; third, accepting his invitations and doing what he commands; fourth, recognizing and rejoicing in the love that he has shown in approaching you and drawing you into this divine fellowship.*

Knowing God is a relationship calculated to thrill a person's heart. What happens is that the almighty Creator, the Lord of hosts, the great God before whom the nations are as a drop in a bucket, comes to you and begins to talk to you through the words and truths of Holy Scripture. Perhaps you have been acquainted with the Bible and Christian truth for many years, and it has meant little to you; but one day you wake up to the fact that God is actually speaking to you—you!—through the biblical message. As you listen to what God is saying, you find yourself brought very low; for God talks to you about your sins, and guilt, and weakness, and blindness, and folly, and compels you to judge yourself hopeless and helpless, and to cry out for forgiveness.

But this is not all. You come to realize as you listen that God is actually opening his heart to you, making friends with you and enlisting you as a colleague. It is a staggering thing, but it is true—the relationship in which sinful human beings know God is one in which God, so to speak, takes them onto his staff, to be henceforth his fellow workers and personal friends.

The almighty God speaks to you, draws you into friendship. Take time to ponder what this means in your life.

PRAY
■ Meeting God

■ *"And the LORD said to Moses, 'I am pleased with you and I know you by name'" (Ex 33:17). "Before I formed you [Jeremiah] in the womb I knew you, before you were born I set you apart" (Jer 1:5). "I am the good shepherd; I know my sheep and my sheep know me . . . and I lay down my life for the sheep" (Jn 10:14-15). What matters supremely is not, in the last analysis, that I know God, but the larger fact that underlies it—the fact that he knows me. I am graven on the palms of his hands.*

Spend a few moments in silence trying to apprehend these truths. Then write a prayerful response to God.

JOURNAL
■ Responding to God

■ *There is, certainly, great cause for humility in the thought that God sees all the twisted things about me that my fellow humans do not see (and I am glad!), and that he sees more corruption in me than I see in myself (which, in all conscience, is enough). There is, however, equally great incentive to worship and love God because, for some unfathomable reason, he wants me as his friend.*

Record below your personal response to this concept. It might take the form of a letter to God, words of a song or hymn, a sketch, or jotted notes of your thoughts.

4

THE ONLY TRUE GOD

READ

■ **An Excerpt from *Knowing God***

■ *What does the word* idolatry *suggest to your mind? Savages groveling before a totem pole? Cruel-faced statues in Hindu temples? The dervish dance of the priests of Baal around Elijah's altar? These things are certainly idolatrous,* in a very obvious way; but we need to realize that there are more subtle forms of idolatry as well.

Look at the second commandment. It runs as follows: "You shall not make for yourself an idol in the form of anything in heaven above or on the earth beneath or in the waters below. You shall not bow down to them or worship them; for I, the LORD your God, am a jealous God" (Ex 20:4-5).

What are some ways you try to obey this command?

What do you think you should avoid in order to obey it?

STUDY
■ Knowing the God of Scripture

Read the first three commandments as recorded in Exodus 20:3-7. In what ways is each of these commands different from the others?

How are these three commands related to each other?

What can you know of God's character from these commands?

What do you see here that would cause you to take these commands seriously?

What particular difficulties do you face when you try to keep these commands?

Read Matthew 22:3-37, Jesus' summary of the first section of the Ten Commandments. Does this summary make it harder or easier for you to obey God? Explain.

 **REFLECT**
■ Understanding the Character of God

■ *The second commandment means that we are not to make use of visual or pictorial representations of the triune God, or of any person of the Trinity, for the purposes of Christian worship. God says quite categorically, "Thou shalt not make any likeness of any thing" for use in worship. This categorical statement rules out not simply the use of pictures and statues which depict God as an animal, but also the use of pictures and statues which depict him as the highest created thing we know—a human. It also rules out the use of pictures and statues of Jesus Christ as a man, although Jesus himself was a man; for all pictures and statues are necessarily made after the "likeness" of manhood as we conceive it, and therefore come under the ban which the commandment imposes.*

Reflect on the statements above as they relate to the Scripture you have studied. Record your thoughts, questions, objections or conclusions in the space below.

PRAY
■ Meeting God

■ *How often do we hear this sort of thing: "I like to think of God as the great Architect (or Mathematician or Artist)." "I don't think of God as a Judge; I like to think of him simply as Father."* We know from experience how often remarks of this kind serve as the prelude to a denial of something that the Bible tells us about God. It needs to be said with the greatest possible emphasis that those who hold themselves free to think of God as they like are breaking the second commandment. At best, they can only think of God in the image of man—as an ideal man, perhaps, or a superman. But God is not any sort of man. We were made in his image, but we must not think of him as existing in ours.

Pray, confessing any sin that relates to thinking of God as the kind of god who is comfortable to you—rather than worshiping him as the God that he declares himself to be. Record some of your prayer below.

JOURNAL
■ Responding to God

■ *The mind that takes up with images is a mind that has not yet learned to love and attend to God's Word. Those who look to manmade images, material or mental, to lead them to God are not likely to take any part of his revelation as seriously as they should.*

Who is God—according to the Bible? Using a concordance or study Bible, write as many biblical descriptions as you can, along with a verifying reference for each one.

God is . . .

5

GOD INCARNATE

READ

■ **An Excerpt from *Knowing God***

■ *It is no wonder that thoughtful people find the gospel of Jesus Christ hard to believe, for the realities with which it deals pass our understanding. . . . The really staggering Christian claim is that Jesus of Nazareth was God made man.*
. . . *Here are two mysteries for the price of one—the plurality of persons within the unity of God, and the union of Godhead and manhood in the person of Jesus. . . . The Almighty appeared on earth as a helpless human baby, unable to do more than lie and stare and wriggle and make noises, needing to be fed and changed and taught to talk like any other child. And there was no illusion or deception in this: the babyhood of the Son of God was a reality. The more you think about it, the more staggering it gets. Nothing in fiction is so fantastic as is this truth of the Incarnation.*

If you could ask God some questions about what exactly happened when Jesus took on human form, what would you ask?

STUDY
■ Knowing the God of Scripture

■ *What does the Bible mean when it calls Jesus the Son of God? John wrote, as he tells us, in order that we might "believe that Jesus is the Christ, the Son of God, and that by believing . . . have life in his name" (Jn 20:31). Hence his famous prologue of John 1:1-18. Nowhere else in the New Testament is the nature and meaning of Jesus' divine Sonship so clearly explained as here.*

Read John 1:1-18. What can you know from verses 1-4 about Jesus, the Word?

What is the function of John the Baptist (vv. 6-9, 15)?

What different responses would various people have to Jesus?

What gifts would Jesus offer those who believed his true identity?

What is your personal response to the incarnation as it is described in John's prologue?

■ *When, therefore, the Bible proclaims Jesus as the Son of God, the statement is meant as an assertion of his distinct personal deity. The Christmas message rests on the staggering fact that the child in the manger was—God.*

REFLECT
■ Understanding the Character of God

"The Word became flesh and made his dwelling among us. We have seen his glory, the glory of the One and Only, who came from the Father, full of grace and truth" (Jn 1:14).

Reflect on these words using the following steps:

☐ Read the verse slowly several times aloud, listening to each phrase.

☐ Study each phrase and the mysteries contained there.

☐ Write your best understanding of what each phrase means.

Keep silent for a few moments, allowing the truths of this verse to seep into your soul.

Read the verse again aloud, then pray. Worship God as seems appropriate based on meditation of this verse.

PRAY
■ Meeting God

■ *The Word had become flesh: a real human baby. He had not ceased to be God; he was no less God then than before, but he had begun to be man. He who made the angel who became the devil was now in a state in which he could be tempted—could not, indeed, avoid being tempted—by the devil; and the perfection of his human life was achieved only by conflict with the devil. The epistle to the Hebrews, looking up to him in his ascended glory, draws great comfort from this fact.*

"He had to be made like his brothers in every way. . . . Because he himself suffered when he was tempted, he is able to help those who are being tempted. . . . For we do not have a high priest who is unable to sympathize with our weaknesses, but we have one who has been tempted in every way, just as we are—yet was without sin. Let us then approach the throne of grace with confidence, so that we may receive mercy and find grace to help us in our time of need" (Heb 2:17-18; 4:15-16).

Pray, bringing to God any particular temptations or weaknesses you feel today. Jesus knows.

JOURNAL
■ Responding to God

Page through a hymnal or worship book looking for songs that speak of the incarnation. When you find one that you particularly like, copy the words, taking particular note of their meaning. Then sing or read them as your own act of worship.

If you need help, look for one of the following:

"Of the Father's Love Begotten," Aurelius Clemens Prudentius, A.D. 348-413.

"And Can It Be That I Should Gain," Charles Wesley, 1738.

"Let All Mortal Flesh Keep Silence," Liturgy of St. James, fifth century.

"Thou Who Wast Rich Beyond All Splendor," Frank Houghton, 1894-1972.

6

HE SHALL TESTIFY

READ

■ An Excerpt from *Knowing God*

■ *Many excellent books have been written about the person and work of Christ, . . . but the average Christian, deep down, is in a complete fog as to what work the Holy Spirit does. . . . Christians are aware of the difference it would make if, after all, it transpired that there had never been an Incarnation or an atonement. They know that then they would be lost, for they would have no Savior. But many Christians have really no idea what difference it would make if there were no Holy Spirit in the world. Whether in that case they, or the church, would suffer in any way they just do not know. Surely something is amiss here.*

Sketch a few quick notes of what you know to be true of the Holy Spirit.

What specifically has been the work of God's Spirit in your life?

STUDY
■ Knowing the God of Scripture

■ *The average Anglican clergyman never preaches on the Trinity except perhaps on Trinity Sunday; the average nonliturgical minister, who does not observe Trinity Sunday, never preaches on it at all. One wonders what the apostle John would say, were he here to comment on our practice. For according to him the doctrine of the Trinity is an essential part of the Christian gospel.*

Read John 14:15-31 and 16:5-15. Make notes of where each person of the Trinity is mentioned.

What do you learn here about the work of each aspect of God's tri-personality?

Father:

Son:

Spirit:

What does this text reveal about the various relationships within the Trinity?

The disciples had just learned that Jesus would be leaving them. What do you see here that would be a comfort to the disciples?

What are some of your own thanksgivings and longings about the Holy Spirit?

REFLECT

■ Understanding the Character of God

■ *Having explained that he was going to prepare a place for them in his Father's house, Jesus went on to promise his disciples the gift of "another Comforter" (Jn 14:16 KJV). Note this phrase; it is full of meaning. It denotes a person, and a remarkable person too. A Comforter—the richness of the idea is seen from the variety of renderings in different translations: "counselor" (RSV), "helper" (Moffatt), "advocate" (Weymouth), one "to befriend you" (Knox). The thoughts of encouragement, support, assistance, care, the shouldering of responsibility for another's welfare, are all conveyed by this word. . . .*

Our Lord went on to name the new Comforter. He is "the Spirit of truth," "the Holy Spirit" (Jn 14:17, 26). This name denoted deity. In the Old Testament, God's word and God's Spirit are parallel figures. God's word is his almighty speech; God's Spirit is his almighty breath. Both phrases convey the thought of his power in action.

Choose one or more of these descriptions of God's Spirit and spend several minutes reflecting on God as he is revealed in that quality. Recall times when you have been conscious of that aspect of God. Make notes on your reflections below.

PRAY
■ **Meeting God**

■ *Do we honor the Holy Spirit by recognizing and relying on his work? Or do we slight him by ignoring it, and thereby dishonor not merely the Spirit but the Lord who sent him?*

Review the qualities of the Holy Spirit as described in the "Reflect" section. Express your thanks and worship in prayer.

JOURNAL
■ Responding to God

In cold-eyed honesty evaluate the honor that you give to the Holy Spirit, using the criteria below. Make notes of your observations.

In my faith: Do I acknowledge the authority of the Bible which he inspired? Do I read and hear it with reverence and receptiveness?

In my life: Do I live by the Bible, whatever anyone may say against it, recognizing that what God has said he certainly means, and he will stand behind it?

In my witness: Do I remember that the Holy Spirit alone, by his witness, can authenticate my witness, and do I trust him to do so?

7

GOD UNCHANGING

READ
- **An Excerpt from *Knowing God***

■ They tell us that the Bible is the Word of God—a lamp to our feet and a light to our path. They tell us that we shall find in it the knowledge of God and of his will for our lives. We believe them; rightly, for what they say is true. So we take our Bibles and start to read. We read steadily and thoughtfully, for we are in earnest; we really do want to know God.

But as we read, we get more and more puzzled. Though fascinated, we are not being fed. Our reading is not helping us; it leaves us bewildered and, if the truth be told, somewhat depressed. We find ourselves wondering whether Bible reading is worth going on with.

What is our trouble? Well, basically it is this. Our Bible reading takes us into what, for us, is quite a new world—namely, the Near Eastern world as it was thousands of years ago, primitive and barbaric, agricultural and unmechanized. It is in that world that the action of the Bible story is played out. . . .

The link is God himself. For the God with whom they had to do is the same God with whom we have to do. We could sharpen the point by saying exactly the same God; for God does not change in the least particular. Thus it appears that the truth on which we must dwell, in order to dispel this feeling that there is an unbridgeable gulf between the position of men and women in Bible times and in our own, is the truth of God's immutability.

Are there any parts of the Bible that have seemed particularly strange and inaccessible to you?

STUDY
■ Knowing the God of Scripture

■ *Created things have a beginning and an ending, but not so their Creator. The answer to the child's question "Who made God?" is simply that God did not need to be made, for he was always there.*

Read Psalm 90. What concepts here cause you to stand in awe of God?

What comparisons do you see between God and humans?

Why is God "from everlasting to everlasting" a good "dwelling place"?

In what ways has God been your own dwelling place?

What prayerful requests in this psalm would you like to make your own?

REFLECT
■ **Understanding the Character of God**

■ God does not change. *Let us draw out this thought.*
1. *God's life* does not change.
2. *God's character* does not change.
3. *God's truth* does not change.
4. *God's ways* do not change.
5. *God's purposes* do not change.
6. *God's Son does* not change.

Do you find the immutability of God comforting? Frightening? Both? Explain.

■ *Note: It is true that there is a group of texts (Gen 6:6-7; 1 Sam 15:11; 2 Sam 24:16; Jn 3:10; Joel 2:13-14) which speak of God as repenting. The reference in each case is to a reversal of God's previous treatment of particular people, consequent upon their reaction to that treatment. But there is no suggestion that this reaction was not foreseen, or that it took God by surprise and was not provided for in his eternal plan. No change in his eternal purpose is implied when he begins to deal with a person in a new way.*

PRAY
■ Meeting God

Look again at Psalm 90. Read it aloud to God as your own prayer of worship.

Record below several phrases from the psalm that you want to come back to as a basis for continued prayer.

JOURNAL
■ **Responding to God**

■ *Where is the sense of distance and difference, then, between believers in Bible times and ourselves? It is excluded. On what grounds? On the grounds that God does not change. Fellowship with him, trust in his word, living by faith, standing on the promises of God, are essentially the same realities for us today as they were for Old and New Testament believers. This thought brings comfort as we enter into the perplexities of each day. Amid all the changes and uncertainties of life in a nuclear age, God and his Christ remain the same—almighty to save.*

Bring to mind a biblical character who might be your spiritual kin. Write a note to that person expressing your similarities.

What can you learn from that person's experience with the same God?

8

THE MAJESTY OF GOD

READ
■ **An Excerpt from** *Knowing God*

■ *The Christian's instincts of trust and worship are stimulated very powerfully by knowledge of the greatness of God. But this is knowledge that Christians today largely lack, and that is one reason why our faith is so feeble and our worship so flabby. We are modern people, and modern people, though we cherish great thoughts of ourselves, have as a rule small thoughts of God. When the person in the church, let alone the person in the street, uses the word God, the thought is rarely of divine majesty.*

Do you agree that the description above represents a common problem among today's Christians?

What examples do you see of this problem in your church and in yourself?

STUDY
■ Knowing the God of Scripture

■ *One step to knowing the majesty of God is to compare him with powers and forces we regard as great. . . . In Isaiah 40, God speaks to people whose mood is the mood of many Christians today—despondent people, cowed people, secretly despairing people; people against whom the tide of events has been running for a very long time; people who have ceased to believe that the cause of Christ can ever prosper again. Now see how God through his prophet reasons with them.*

Read Isaiah 40. This chapter opens with the words "Comfort, comfort my people, says your God." What do you find here that comforts you?

What phrases do you see that help you reflect on God's greatness?

How do these forces, as described in Isaiah 40, contrast with God: workers (vv. 10-14), nations (vv. 15-17), great leaders (vv. 23-24), stars (vv. 25-26), all humans (whole chapter)?

How can this chapter help you to better worship God?

REFLECT
■ Understanding the Character of God

■ *Today vast stress is laid on the thought that God is personal, but this truth is so stated as to leave the impression that God is a person of the same sort as we are—weak, inadequate, ineffective, a little pathetic. But this is not the God of the Bible! Our personal life is a finite thing: it is limited in every direction, in space, in time, in knowledge, in power. But God is not so limited. He is eternal, infinite and almighty. He has us in his hands; we never have him in ours. Like us, he is personal; but unlike us, he is great. In all its constant stress on the reality of God's personal concern for his people, and on the gentleness, tenderness, sympathy, patience and yearning compassion that he shows toward them, the Bible never lets us lose sight of his majesty and his unlimited dominion over all his creatures.*

God is both personal and majestic. Which would you say that you emphasize most? (Consider your thinking, prayers and worship.)

What steps could you take to achieve a more biblical balance?

PRAY
■ Meeting God

Read Isaiah 40 again, asking God to lead you into prayer through your reading. As a phrase or concept seems particularly appropriate, stop and pray. Record some of these phrases and your prayers below.

Those who hope in the LORD
  will renew their strength.
They will soar on wings like eagles;
  they will run and not grow weary,
  they will walk and not faint. (Is 40:31)

JOURNAL
■ **Responding to God**

■ *Let Isaiah now apply to us the Bible doctrine of the majesty of God by asking us the three questions that he puts in God's name to the disillusioned and downcast Israelites.* Journal your own answers to these questions.

1. "To whom will you compare me, that I should be like him? says the Holy One" (Is 40:25 RSV). This question rebukes *wrong thoughts about God.*

2. "Why sayest thou, O Jacob, and speakest, O Israel, My way is hid from the Lord and my judgment is passed over from my God?" (Is 40:27 KJV). This question rebukes *wrong thoughts about ourselves.*

3. "Hast thou not known? hast thou not heard, *that* the everlasting God, the LORD, the Creator of the ends of the earth, fainteth not, neither is weary?" (Is 40:28 KJV). This question rebukes *our slowness to believe in God's majesty.*

9

GOD ONLY WISE

READ
■ **An Excerpt from *Knowing God***

■ *Wisdom is the power to see, and the inclination to choose, the best and the highest goal, together with the surest means of attaining it. Wisdom is, in fact, the practical side of moral goodness. As such, it is found in its fullness only in God. He alone is naturally and entirely and invariably wise.*

Spend a few moments reflecting on God's wisdom as you have seen it demonstrated and as you trust it to be true even when you cannot see its evidence.

Talk to God about these reflections.

STUDY
■ Knowing the God of Scripture

■ *Young Joseph's brothers sold him into slavery in Egypt where, traduced by Potiphar's venomous wife, he was wrongly imprisoned, though afterward he rose to eminence. For what purpose did God in his wisdom plan that? So far as Joseph personally was concerned, the answer is given in Psalm 105:19: "the word of the LORD tried him" (KJV).*

Read Genesis 50:15-21. (If you are unfamiliar with Joseph's story, read all of Genesis 37—50.) What reasons did Joseph's brothers have to be afraid?

In what ways was Joseph's response to them different from what they expected or deserved?

How did Joseph demonstrate his faith in the wisdom of God?

What does Joseph's response suggest about the way he viewed his years of pain?

■ *Note: Joseph's theology was as sound as his charity was deep. Through him we are confronted with the wisdom of God ordering the events of a human life for a double purpose: the individual's own personal sanctification, and the fulfilling of his appointed ministry and service in the life of the people of God.*

REFLECT
■ Understanding the Character of God

■ *Wisdom without power would be pathetic, a broken reed; power without wisdom would be merely frightening; but in God boundless wisdom and endless power are united, and this makes him utterly worthy of our fullest trust. . . . Misunderstanding what the Bible means when it says that God is love (see 1 Jn 4:8-10), people sometimes think that God intends a trouble-free life for all, irrespective of their moral and spiritual state, and hence they conclude that anything painful and upsetting (illness, accident, injury, loss of job, the suffering of a loved one) indicates either that God's wisdom, or power, or both, have broken down, or that God, after all, does not exist.*

But this idea of God's intention is a complete mistake: God's wisdom is not, and never was, pledged to keep a fallen world happy, or to make ungodliness comfortable. Not even to Christians has he promised a trouble-free life; rather the reverse. He has other ends in view for life in this world than simply to make it easy for everyone.

What is he after, then? What is his goal? What does he aim at? When he made us, his purpose was that we should love and honor him, praising him for the wonderfully ordered complexity and variety of his world, using it according to his will, and so enjoying both it and him. . . . He plans that a great host of humankind should come to love and honor him, . . . he and they rejoicing continually in the knowledge of each other's love. . . . This will be God's glory, and our glory too. . . . But it will only be fully realized in the next world.

Think of one way in which you have begun to taste the "glory" that God's wisdom has purposed for you. Take time to savor this gift.

PRAY
■ Meeting God

■ *How are we to meet these baffling and trying situations, if we cannot for the moment see God's purpose in them? First, by taking them as from God, and asking ourselves what reactions to them, and in them, the gospel of God requires of us; second, by seeking God's face specifically about them.*

Talk to God (in writing) about the hard and baffling events of your life. As much as you are able, express your trust in his wisdom.

JOURNAL
■ Responding to God

■ *We may be frankly bewildered at things that happen to us, but God knows exactly what he is doing, and what he is after, in his handling of our affairs. Always, and in everything, he is wise: we shall see that hereafter, even where we never saw it here.*

Record below some of the events of your life that you find bewildering.

■ *Note: Job in heaven knows the full reason he was afflicted, though he never knew it in this life.*

10

GOD'S WISDOM AND OURS

READ

■ **An Excerpt from** *Knowing God*

■ *Rarely does this world look as if a beneficent Providence were running it. Rarely does it appear that there is a rational power behind it at all. Often what is worthless survives, while what is valuable perishes. . . . Yet we feel that, for the honor of God (and also, though we do not say this, for the sake of our own reputation as spiritual Christians), it is necessary for us to claim that we are . . . here and now enjoying inside information as to the why and wherefore of God's doings. This comforting pretense becomes part of us: we feel sure that God has enabled us to understand all his ways with us and our circle thus far, and we take it for granted that we shall be able to see at once the reason for anything that may happen to us in the future.*

And then something very painful and quite inexplicable comes along.

When has this been your experience?

How has that experience challenged your sense of knowing God?

STUDY
■ Knowing the God of Scripture

Be realistic, says the preacher of Ecclesiastes; face facts; see life as it is. You will have no true wisdom till you do. The book of Ecclesiastes tells of an experiment. How is a person to find meaning in life? Is this possible? While much of the book is a search through dead ends, the "preacher" comes to several wise conclusions. What can you know of true wisdom from the passages below?

3:9-14:

5:1-7:

7:14:

9:7-10:

11:1-6:

12:1:

12:13-14:

REFLECT
■ Understanding the Character of God

■ *Among the seven deadly sins of medieval lore was sloth (acedia)—a state of hard-bitten, joyless apathy of spirit. There is a lot of it around today in Christian circles; the symptoms are personal spiritual inertia [and] critical cynicism. . . . Behind this morbid and deadening condition often lies the wounded pride of one who thought he knew all about the ways of God in providence and then was made to learn by bitter and bewildering experience that he didn't. This is what happens when we do not heed the message of Ecclesiastes. For the truth is that God in his wisdom, to make and keep us humble and to teach us to walk by faith, has hidden from us almost everything that we should like to know about the providential purposes which he is working out in the churches and in our own lives. "As thou knowest not what is the way of the wind, nor how the bones do grow in the womb of her that is with child; even so thou knowest not the work of God who doeth all" (11:5 RV).*

Would you say that your own painful experiences have led you to wisdom or cynicism? Explain.

PRAY
■ Meeting God

■ *What is the wisdom that God gives? . . . It is not a sharing in all his knowledge, but a disposition to confess that he is wise, and to cleave to him and live for him in the light of his Word through thick and thin. Thus the effect of his gift of wisdom is to make us more humble, more joyful, more godly, more quicksighted as to his will, more resolute in the doing of it and less troubled (not less sensitive, but less bewildered) than we were at the dark and painful things of which our life in this fallen world is full.*

Bring to mind some of the dark and painful things of your own life—and ask for this kind of wisdom from God.

If any of you lacks wisdom, he should ask of God, who gives generously to all without finding fault, and it will be given to him. (Jas 1:5)

JOURNAL
■ Responding to God

■ *We can trust in God and rejoice in him, even when we cannot discern his path. Thus the preacher's way of wisdom boils down to what was expressed by Richard Baxter:*

Ye *saints, who toil below,*
  Adore your heavenly King,
And onward as ye go
  Some joyful anthem sing.
Take what He gives,
  And praise Him still
Through good and ill
  Who ever lives.

Create your own statement of trust in God—even for times when you cannot understand his ways.

11

THY WORD IS TRUTH

READ

■ **An Excerpt from** *Knowing God*

■ *An absolute ruler, such as all kings were in the ancient world, will in the ordinary course of things speak regularly on two levels and for two purposes. On the one hand, he will enact regulations and laws which directly determine the environment—judicial, fiscal, cultural—within which his subjects must henceforth live. On the other hand, he will make public speeches in order to establish, as far as possible, a personal link between himself and his subjects. . . . The Bible pictures the word of God as having a similar twofold character. God is the king; we, his creatures, are his subjects. His word relates both to things around us and to us directly: God speaks both to determine our environment and to engage our minds and hearts.*

In the former connection, which is the sphere of creation and providence, God's word takes the form of a sovereign fiat: "Let there be . . ." But the word which God addresses directly to us is . . . not only of government, but also of fellowship. For, though God is a great king, it is not his wish to live at a distance from his subjects. Rather the reverse: He made us with the intention that he and we might walk together forever in a love relationship.

When have you been impressed with God's word as a large system under his rule?

When have you been impressed with God's word as an invitation to deep relationship?

STUDY
■ Knowing the God of Scripture

Read John 17:1-26, Jesus' prayer for his disciples and all future believers—including us. What do you see here that suggests that God is ruler of the universe?

What do you see here that suggests God's desire for relationship with his people?

What can you know from verses 13-18 about God's word?

In verse 17 Jesus says to his Father, "Your word is truth." How is this different from any other form of truth that you know?

Read again the section of the prayer for all believers (vv. 20-26). What are you particularly thankful for here?

REFLECT
■ Understanding the Character of God

■ *What is a Christian? Christians can be described from many angles, but . . . we can cover everything by saying: True Christians are people who acknowledge and live under the word of God. They submit without reserve to the word of God written in "the book of Truth" (Dan 10:21), believing the teaching, trusting the promises, following the commands. Their eyes are upon the God of the Bible as their Father and the Christ of the Bible as their Savior.*

Christians will tell you, if you ask them, that the Word of God has both convinced them of sin and assured them of forgiveness. . . . They aspire, like the psalmist, to have their whole lives brought into line with it. . . . The promises are before them as they pray, and the precepts are before them as they go about their daily tasks.

Christians know that in addition to the word of God spoken directly to them in the Scriptures, God's word has gone forth to create, and control, and order things around them; but since the Scriptures tell them that all things work together for their good, the thought of God's ordering their circumstances brings them only joy. Christians are independent folks, for they use the Word of God as a touchstone by which to test the various views that are put to them, and they will not touch anything which they are not sure that Scripture sanctions.

Why does this description fit so few of us who profess to be Christians in these days? You will find it profitable to ask your conscience, and let it tell you.

As "various views" are put to you, do portions of God's Word come to mind to help you put these views to the test?

What is one step you could take to saturate yourself more deeply in Scripture?

PRAY
■ Meeting God

Read again Jesus' prayer for you in John 17:20-26. Write your own prayer of response.

JOURNAL
■ Responding to God

Study the description of a Christian in the "Reflect" section. Probe your conscience as the final paragraph asks. Then write your observations below.

12

THE LOVE OF GOD

READ
■ An Excerpt from *Knowing God*

■ *John's twice-repeated statement, "God is love" (1 Jn 4:8, 16), is one of the most tremendous utterances of the Bible— and also one of the most misunderstood. False ideas have grown up round it like a hedge of thorns, hiding its real meaning from view, and it is no small task cutting through this tangle of mental undergrowth. Yet the hard thought involved is more than repaid when the true sense of these texts comes home to the Christian soul. Those who climb Scotland's Ben Nevis do not complain of their labor once they see the view from the top! . . .*

When we looked at God's wisdom, we saw something of his mind; when we thought of his power, we saw something of his hand and his arm; when we considered his word, we learned about his mouth; but now, contemplating his love, we are to look into his heart. We shall stand on holy ground; we need the grace of reverence, that we may tread it without sin.

Pray for that "grace of reverence" as you begin this study.

STUDY
■ **Knowing the God of Scripture**

Read 1 John 4:7-21. Describe God's love as John reveals it.

In what ways does God show his love to us, according to this passage?

If God's love is in us, what are some ways that this will become obvious?

Verse 19 says, "We love because he [God] first loved us." What does this mean?

Verse 18 says, "Perfect love drives out fear." How might this passage help you to approach God with some measure of confidence?

What are some specific ways in which you would like to reflect God's love for you?

REFLECT

■ Understanding the Character of God

■ *God who is love is first and foremost light, and sentimental ideas of his love as an indulgent, benevolent softness, divorced from moral standards and concerns, must therefore be ruled out from the start. God's love is holy love. The God whom Jesus made known is not a God who is indifferent to moral distinctions, but a God who loves righteousness and hates iniquity, a God whose ideal for his children is that they should "be perfect . . . as your heavenly Father is perfect" (Mt 5:48). He will not take into his company any person, however orthodox in mind, who will not follow after holiness of life. . . .*

But just as God is light in everything he says and does, so also God is love in everything he says and does. . . . Thus, so far as we are concerned, God is love to us—holy, omnipotent love—at every moment and in every event of every day's life. Even when we cannot see the why and the wherefore of God's dealings, we know that there is love in and behind them, and so we can rejoice always, even when, humanly speaking, things are going wrong. We know that the true story of our life, when known, will prove to be, as the hymn says, "mercy from first to last"—and we are content. . . .

Definition: God's love is an exercise of his goodness toward individual sinners whereby, having identified himself with their welfare, he has given his Son to be their Savior, and now brings them to know and enjoy him in a covenant relationship.

We often speak of God's "unconditional love." Can God's love be both unconditional and holy? Why or why not?

PRAY
■ Meeting God

The apostle Paul prayed that his friends at Ephesus would grow deeper into God's love:

> For this reason I kneel before the Father, from whom his whole family in heaven and on earth derives its name. I pray that out of his glorious riches he may strengthen you with power through his Spirit in your inner being, so that Christ may dwell in your hearts through faith. And I pray that you, being rooted and established in love, may have power, together with all the saints, to grasp how wide and long and high and deep is the love of Christ, and to know this love that surpasses knowledge— that you may be filled to the measure of all the fullness of God. (Eph 3:14-19)

Pray this prayer of blessing for people you know and love, inserting a new name each time you read the prayer.

JOURNAL
■ Responding to God

John wrote that "God is love" in order to make an ethical point: "Since God so loved us, we also ought to love one another" (1 Jn 4:11). Could an observer learn from the quality and degree of love that I show to others—my wife, my husband, my family, my neighbors, people at church, people at work—anything at all about the greatness of God's love to me?

Meditate on these things. Examine yourself. Record your thoughts below.

13

THE GRACE OF GOD

READ
■ **An Excerpt from** *Knowing God*

■ *It is commonplace in all the churches to call Christianity a religion of grace. . . . But many church people . . . pay lip service to the idea of grace, but there they stop. Their conception of grace is not so much debased as nonexistent. The thought means nothing to them; it does not touch their experience at all. Talk to them about the church's heating, or last year's accounts, and they are with you at once; but speak to them about the realities to which the word* grace *points, and their attitude is one of deferential blankness. . . . What is it that hinders so many who profess to believe in grace from really doing so?*

Note some of your own answers to the above question.

STUDY
■ Knowing the God of Scripture

■ *Paul refers to God's plan of grace in several places, but his fullest account of it is in the massive paragraph—for, despite subdivisions, the flow of thought constitutes essentially one paragraph—running from Ephesians 1:3 to 2:10.*

Read Ephesians 1:3—2:10. Paul opens this paragraph by saying, "God . . . has blessed us in the heavenly realms with every spiritual blessing in Christ." What blessings do you find in this massive passage?

Focus on Ephesians 2:1-10. What actions (past, present and future) do you see God doing in this section?

What is the human condition during each stage of God's work?

Verse 8 speaks of God's grace as a gift from God. What evidence do you see here to support that description?

Verse 10 speaks of works: ours and God's. What is the relationship between the two?

"There have always been some who have found the thought of grace so overwhelmingly wonderful that they could not get over it." What do you find overwhelmingly wonderful about the grace described in Ephesians?

REFLECT
■ Understanding the Character of God

■ *The grace of God is love freely shown toward guilty sinners, contrary to their merit and indeed in defiance of their demerit. It is God showing goodness to persons who deserve only severity and had no reason to expect anything but severity. . . . Now we have to ask, why should this thought mean so much? The answer is not far to seek. . . . It is surely clear that, once a person is convinced that his state and need are as described, the New Testament gospel of grace cannot but sweep him off his feet with wonder and joy. For it tells how our Judge has become our Savior. . . .*

1. Grace as the source of pardon of sin. The gospel centers upon justification—that is, upon the remission of sins and the acceptance of our persons that goes with it. Justification is the truly dramatic transition from the status of a condemned criminal awaiting a terrible sentence to that of an heir awaiting a fabulous inheritance. . . .

2. Grace as the motive of the plan of salvation. Pardon is the heart of the gospel, but it is not the whole doctrine of grace. For the New Testament sets God's gift of pardon in the context of a plan of salvation began with election before the world was and will be completed only when the church is perfect in glory. . . .

3. Grace as the guarantee of the preservation of the saints. If the plan of salvation is certain of accomplishment, then the Christian's future is assured. I am, and will be, "kept by the power of God through faith unto salvation" (1 Pet 1:5 KJV). I need not torment myself with the fear that my faith may fail; as grace led me to faith in the first place, so grace will keep me believing to the end. Faith, both in its origin and continuance, is a gift of grace.

Which of these three meanings of grace has taken deepest root in your life? Which would you like to understand more fully?

PRAY
■ Meeting God

■ *Oh! to grace how great a debtor*
   Daily I'm constrained to be;
   Let that grace now, like a fetter,
      Bind my wandering heart to Thee!
Prone to wander, Lord, I feel it;
   Prone to leave the God I love—
Take my heart, oh, take and seal it,
   Seal it for Thy courts above!

Robert Robinson, 1758

If this is your prayer, use the words above to sing or say your worship to God. Then continue your prayer in the space below.

JOURNAL
■ Responding to God

■ *The reaction of the Christian heart contemplating all this, comparing how things were with how they are in consequence of the appearing of grace in the world, was given supreme expression by the one-time president of Princeton, Samuel Davies:*

Great God of wonders! all thy ways
*   Display the attributes divine;*
But countless acts of pardoning grace
*   Beyond thine other wonders shine:*
Who is a pardoning God like Thee?
Or who has grace so rich and free?

In wonder lost, with trembling joy,
*   We take the pardon of our God;*
Pardon for crimes of deepest dye,
*   A pardon bought with Jesus' blood:*
Who is a pardoning God like Thee?
Or who has grace so rich and free?

Reflect on God's grace by creating additional stanzas to this hymn.

14

GOD THE JUDGE

READ
■ An Excerpt from *Knowing God*

■ *Do you believe in divine judgment? By which I mean, do you believe in a God who acts as our Judge?*

Many, it seems, do not. Speak to them of God as a Father, a friend, a helper, one who loves us despite all our weakness and folly and sin, and their faces light up; you are on their wavelength at once. But speak to them as Judge and they frown and shake their heads. Their minds recoil from such an idea. They find it repellent and unworthy.

What is your own reaction to the thought of God as Judge? (Make notes below.)

STUDY
■ Knowing the God of Scripture

Study the passages below. What does each passage teach about God as judge?

Daniel 5:5-6, 23-30:

Matthew 12:35-37:

Matthew 25:31-46:

John 5:25-30:

Acts 5:1-10:

Acts 17:30-31:

Romans 2:5-6:

2 Corinthians 5:10:

Hebrews 12:22-24:

Revelation 20:11-15:

REFLECT

■ Understanding the Character of God

■ *Why do we fight shy of the thought of God as a Judge? Why do we feel the thought to be unworthy of him? The truth is that part of God's moral perfection is his perfection in judgment. Would a God who did not care about the difference between right and wrong be a good and admirable Being? Would a God who put no distinction between the beasts of history, the Hitlers and Stalins (if we dare use names), and his own saints, be morally praiseworthy and perfect? Moral indifference would be an imperfection in God, not a perfection. But not to judge the world would be to show moral indifference. The final proof that God is a perfect moral Being, not indifferent to questions of right and wrong, is the fact that he has committed himself to judge the world.*

It is clear that the reality of divine judgment must have a direct effect on our view of life. If we know that retributive judgment faces us at the end of the road, we shall not live as otherwise we would. But it must be emphasized that the doctrine of divine judgment, and particularly of the final judgment, is not to be thought of primarily as a bogey with which to frighten men into an outward form of conventional "righteousness." It has its frightening implications for godless men, it is true; but its main thrust is as a revelation of the moral character of God, and an imparting of moral significance to human life.

What comfort, even joy, can you take in the fact that God is not "morally indifferent"? Where do you see a need for judgment, for setting things right, in yourself and in the world around you?

PRAY
■ Meeting God

■ *Paul refers to the fact that we must all appear before Christ's judgment seat as "the terror of the Lord" (2 Cor 5:11 KJV), and well he might. Jesus the Lord, like his Father, is holy and pure; we are neither. We live under his eye, he knows our secrets, and on judgment day the whole of our past life will be played back, as it were, before him, and brought under review. If we know ourselves at all, we know we are not fit to face him. What then are we to do? The New Testament answer is: Call on the coming Judge to be your present Savior. . . . You will then discover that you are looking forward to that future meeting with joy, knowing that there is "no condemnation for those who are in Christ Jesus" (Rom 8:1).*

Write a prayer telling God your worries or joys about this coming meeting.

JOURNAL
■ Responding to God

■ *Final judgment will be according to our works—that is, our doings, our whole course of life. The relevance of our doings is not that they ever merit an award from the court— they fall too far short of perfection to do that—but that they provide an index of what is in the heart—what, in other words, is the real nature of each person. What is the significance of that? It is not that one way of acting is meritorious while the other is not, but that from our actions can be seen whether there is love to Christ, the love that springs from faith, in the heart.*

Bring to mind one of the more troublesome areas of your life. In what ways do you hope that your actions in that setting will show the commitment to Christ that is in your heart?

15

THE WRATH OF GOD

READ

■ **An Excerpt from *Knowing God***

■ *To an age that has unashamedly sold itself to the gods of greed, pride, sex and self-will, the church mumbles on about God's kindness but says virtually nothing about his judgment. How often during the past year did you hear, or, if you are a minister, did you preach, a sermon on the wrath of God? How long is it, I wonder, since a Christian spoke straight on this subject on radio or television, or in one of those half-column sermonettes that appear in some national dailies and magazines? (And if one did so, how long would it be before he would be asked to speak or write again?) The fact is that the subject of divine wrath has become taboo in modern society, and Christians by and large have accepted the taboo and conditioned themselves never to raise the matter.*

When you think of the wrath of God, what images come to mind?

What worries or frightens you about God's wrath?

STUDY
■ **Knowing the God of Scripture**

■ *One cannot imagine that talk of divine judgment was ever very popular, yet the biblical writers engage in it constantly. One of the most striking things about the Bible is the vigor with which both Testaments emphasize the reality and terror of God's wrath.*

Read Nahum 1:2-6 and Romans 1:28—2:6. According to these passages, what are some ways in which God reveals his wrath?

What brings on God's wrath?

In view of these descriptions of God's wrath, what reasons do we have to fear him?

Would you say that the wrath of God, as described in these passages, is deserved or undeserved? Why?

What signs do you see of God's kindness (or fairness) even in passages speaking of his wrath?

How does God's wrath affect your relationship with him?

REFLECT
■ Understanding the Character of God

■ *Clearly, the theme of God's wrath is one about which bibli-cal writers feel no inhibitions whatever. Why, then, should we? . . . The root cause of our unhappiness seems to be a dis-quieting suspicion that ideas of wrath are in one way or another unworthy of God. To some, for instance, wrath suggests a loss of self-control, an outburst of "seeing red" that is partly if not wholly irratio-nal. To others it suggests the rage of conscious impotence, or wounded pride or plain bad temper. Surely, it is said, it would be wrong to ascribe to God such attitudes as these? . . .*

But in the Bible God's wrath is always judicial—that is, it is the wrath of the Judge, administering justice. Cruelty is always immoral, but the explicit presupposition of all that we find in the Bible . . . on the torments of those who experience the fullness of God's wrath is that each receives pre-cisely what he deserves. "The day of God's wrath," Paul tells us, . . . is also the day "when his righteous judgment will be revealed. God 'will give to each person according to what he has done'" (Rom 2:5-6). . . .

In the second place, God's wrath in the Bible is something which people choose for themselves. Before hell is an experience inflicted by God, it is a state for which a person himself opts by retreating from the light that God shines in his heart to lead him to himself. . . . All that God does subse-quently in judicial action toward the unbeliever, whether in this life or beyond it, is to show him, and lead him into, the full implications of the choice he has made.

When have you experienced anger—your own or others'—as destructive? Have you ever experienced it as a force for good?

How is God's wrath, as revealed in Scripture, similar to these in-stances of human anger? How is it different?

PRAY

■ **Meeting God**

■ *Is there any way of deliverance, then, from the wrath to come? There is, and Paul knows it. "Since we have now been justified by his blood," Paul proclaims, "how much more shall we be saved from God's wrath through him!" (Rom 5:9). By whose blood? The blood of Jesus Christ, the incarnate Son of God. And what does it mean to be justified? It means to be forgiven and accepted as righteous. And how do we come to be justified? Through faith—that is, self-abandoning trust in the person and work of Jesus. And how does Jesus' blood—that is, his sacrificial death—form a basis for our justification? Paul explains this in Romans 3:24-25, where he speaks of "the redemption that is in Christ Jesus: whom God hath set forth to be a propitiation through faith in his blood" (KJV). What is a propitiation? It is a sacrifice that averts wrath through expiating sin and canceling guilt. . . .*

This is the real heart of the gospel: that Jesus Christ, by virtue of his death on the cross as our substitute and sinbearer, "is the propitiation for our sins" (1 Jn 2:2 KJV). Between us sinners and the thunderclouds of divine wrath stands the cross of the Lord Jesus. If we are Christ's, though faith, then we are justified through his cross, and the wrath will never touch us, neither here nor hereafter. Jesus "delivers us from the wrath to come" (1 Thess 1:10 RSV).

Pray your own thanks for this gift.

JOURNAL
■ Responding to God

The wrath of God is perfection of the Divine character on which we need to meditate frequently. . . . [To do so will] draw out our soul in fervent praise [to Jesus Christ] for having delivered us from "the wrath to come" (1 Thess. 1:10). Our readiness or our reluctancy to meditate upon the wrath of God becomes a sure test of how our hearts really stand affected towards Him. (A. W. Pink, *The Attributes of God*, p. 77)

Spend time meditating on the wrath of God; then write some of your thoughts below.

16

GOODNESS AND SEVERITY

READ

■ **An Excerpt from** *Knowing God*

■ *"Behold therefore the goodness and severity of God,"* *writes Paul in Romans 11:22 (KJV). The crucial word here is and. . . . The Christians at Rome are not to dwell on God's goodness alone, nor on his severity alone, but to contemplate both together. Both are attributes of God—aspects, that is, of his revealed character. Both appear alongside each other in the economy of grace. Both must be acknowledged together if God is to be truly known.*

Why is it difficult to think of God's goodness and severity at the same time?

Why do you think this might be important?

STUDY
■ Knowing the God of Scripture

Read Romans 11:17-22. What reasons did the Roman readers have to focus on God's goodness?

What were the Roman readers to do and not to do? Why?

In view of this passage, what can you thank God for?

Verse 20 says that we are to "be afraid." What ought you to fear?

Verse 22 speaks of both God's kindness and God's sternness. What difference would it make if God possessed one but not the other?

REFLECT
■ **Understanding the Character of God**

■ *"Santa Claus theology" carries within itself the seeds of its own collapse, for it cannot cope with the fact of evil. It is no accident that when belief in the "good God" of liberalism became widespread, about the turn of the twentieth century, the so-called problem of evil (which was not regarded as a problem before) suddenly leaped into prominence as the number one concern of Christian apologetics. This was inevitable, for it is not possible to see the good will of a heavenly Santa Claus in heart-breaking destructive things like cruelty, or marital infidelity, or death on the road, or lung cancer. The only way to save the liberal view of God is to dissociate him from these things and to deny that he has any direct relation to them or control over them; in other words, to deny his omnipotence and lordship over his world. Liberal theologians took this course seventy years ago, and the man on the street takes it today. Thus he is left with a kind God who means well but cannot always insulate his children from trouble and grief. When trouble comes, therefore, there is nothing to do but grin and bear it. In this way, by an ironic paradox, faith in a God who is all goodness and no severity tends to confirm men in a fatalistic and pessimistic attitude to life.*

Take a mental survey of your own patterns of prayer. To what extent does your praying reflect a "Santa Claus theology"?

What adjustments could you make in your praying that would reflect a fuller theology of God?

PRAY
■ Meeting God

■ *"You stand fast only through faith. So do not become proud, but stand in awe. For if God did not spare the natural branches, neither will he spare you" (Rom 11:20-21 RSV). The principle which Paul is applying here is that behind every display of divine goodness stands a threat of severity in judgment if that goodness is scorned. If we do not let it draw us to God in gratitude and responsive love, we have only ourselves to blame when God turns against us.*

Consider this warning, then respond in prayer.

The LORD is compassionate and gracious,
    slow to anger, abounding in love. (Ps 103:8)

 JOURNAL
■ **Responding to God**

■ *Within the cluster of God's moral perfections there is one in particular to which the term goodness points. . . . This is the quality of generosity. Generosity means a disposition to give to others in a way which has no mercenary motive and is not limited by what the recipients deserve but consistently goes beyond it. Generosity expresses the simple wish that others should have what they need to make them happy. Generosity is, so to speak, the focal point of God's moral perfection; it is the quality which determines how all God's other excellencies are to be displayed.*

List ways in which God has shown you his generosity.

List several ways in which you want to consider modeling God's generosity in your own life.

17

THE JEALOUS GOD

READ
■ **An Excerpt from *Knowing God***

■ *"The jealous God"—doesn't it sound offensive? For we know jealousy, the green-eyed monster, as a vice, one of the most cancerous and soul-destroying vices that there is; whereas God, we are sure, is perfectly good. How, then, could anyone ever imagine that jealousy is found in him?*

Sketch some of your own answers to this question.

How might you try to reconcile God's jealousy and his compassion?

STUDY

■ Knowing the God of Scripture

Notice the use of the term *jealous* (or related terms like *envy* or *zealous*) in these passages.

What does each passage reveal about God's character?

What personal warning can you take from each?

Exodus 20:3-7:

James 4:4-5:

Ezekiel 39:25:

Isaiah 42:8:

Isaiah 48:10-11:

1 Corinthians 10:21-22:

REFLECT
■ **Understanding the Character of God**

■ *What is the nature of this divine jealousy? How can jealousy be a virtue in God when it is a vice in humans? God's perfections are matter for praise—but how can we praise God for being jealous?*

The answer to these questions will be found if we bear in mind two facts. . . .

First, we have to remember that man is not the measure of his Maker, and that when the language of human personal life is used of God, none of the limitations of human creaturehood are thereby being implied—limited knowledge, or power, or foresight, or strength, or consistency, or anything of that kind. . . . So God's jealousy is not a compound of frustration, envy and spite, as human jealousy so often is, but appears instead as a (literally) praiseworthy zeal to preserve something supremely precious. . . .

Second, vicious jealousy is an expression of the attitude, "I want what you've got, and I hate you because I haven't got it." . . . But there is another sort of jealousy: zeal to protect a love relationship or to avenge it when broken. This jealousy also operates in the sphere of sex; there, however, it appears not as the blind reaction of wounded pride but as the fruit of marital affection. As Professor Tasker has written, married persons "who felt no jealousy at the intrusion of a lover or an adulterer into their home would surely be lacking in moral perception; for the exclusiveness of marriage is the essence of marriage" (The Epistle of James, *p. 106). This sort of jealousy is a positive virtue. . . . Scripture consistently views God's jealousy as being . . . an aspect of this kind of covenant love for his own people.*

What does it mean to you that God feels a pure and loving jealousy for you?

PRAY
■ Meeting God

■ *What, now, of us? Does zeal for the house of God, the cause of God, eat us up?—possess us?—consume us? Can we say with the Master, "My food is to do the will of him who sent me and to finish his work" (Jn 4:34)? What sort of discipleship is ours? Have we not need to pray with that flaming evangelist, George Whitefield—a man as humble as he was zealous—"Lord help me to begin to begin."*

How many of our churches today are sound, respectable—and lukewarm? What, then, must Christ's word be to them? What have we to hope for?—unless, by the mercy of the God who in wrath remembers mercy, we find zeal to repent? Revive us, Lord, before judgment falls!

Use each of the two paragraphs above as a starting point for your own prayer.

JOURNAL
■ Responding to God

■ *God's jealousy leads him, on the one hand, to judge and destroy the faithless among his people who fall into idolatry and sin, and indeed to judge the enemies of righteousness and mercy everywhere. . . . What is it that motivates these actions? Simply the fact that he is "jealous for [his] holy name" (Ezek 39:25 KJV). His name is his nature and character as Jehovah, the LORD, ruler of history, guardian of righteousness and savior of sinners—and God means his name to be known, honored and praised.*

Fill this space with various names of God. Meditate on what each reveals about his being.

How do you use God's name? with reverence and awe? as a joke or an oath? rarely at all? Pray about your answer.

18

THE HEART OF THE GOSPEL

READ
■ **An Excerpt from** *Knowing God*

Prince Paris had carried off Princess Helen to Troy. The Greek expeditionary force had taken ship to recover her, but was held up halfway by persistent contrary winds. Agamemnon, the Greek general, sent home for his daughter and ceremonially slaughtered her as a sacrifice to mollify the evidently hostile gods. The move paid off; west winds blew again, and the fleet reached Troy without further difficulty.

This bit of the Trojan war legend, which dates from about 1000 B.C., mirrors an idea of propitiation on which pagan religion all over the world, and in every age, has been built.

But in the Christian religion, propitiation takes a different twist—one full of grace. The Bible insists that it was God himself who took the initiative in quenching his own wrath against those whom, despite their ill-desert, he loved and had chosen to save.

What do you find troubling about the concept of propitiation?

What do you find hopeful about it?

STUDY
■ Knowing the God of Scripture

Read Hebrews 2:10—3:1. In what ways is this description of God's work similar to the Agamemnon story? How is it different?

What words and phrases here suggest a sense of belonging to God?

Why, according to this passage, did Jesus become human (2:14—3:1)?

How does this passage help you to describe the work of God on your behalf?

What do you find in this text that guides your response to this work of God?

REFLECT
■ Understanding the Character of God

What does the phrase "a propitiation . . . by his blood" (Rom 3:25) express? It expresses, in the context of Paul's argument, precisely this thought: that by his sacrificial death for our sins Christ pacified the wrath of God. . . .

The gospel tells us that our Creator has become our Redeemer. It announces that the Son of God has become man "for us men and for our salvation" and has died on the cross to save us from eternal judgment. The basic description of the saving death of Christ in the Bible is as a propitiation, that is, as that which quenched God's wrath against us by obliterating our sins from his sight. God's wrath is his righteousness reacting against unrighteousness; it shows itself in retributive justice. But Jesus Christ has shielded us from the nightmare prospect of retributive justice by becoming our representative substitute, in obedience to his Father's will, and receiving the wages of our sin in our place.

By this means justice has been done, for the sins of all that will ever be pardoned were judged and punished in the person of God the Son, and it is on this basis that pardon is now offered to us offenders. Redeeming love and retributive justice joined hands, so to speak, at Calvary, for there God showed himself to be "just, and the justifier of him that hath faith in Jesus."

Do you understand this? If you do, you are now seeing to the very heart of the Christian gospel.

Are you coming closer to "seeing to the very heart" of the gospel? What response does it stir in you?

PRAY
■ Meeting God

The book of Revelation shows a scene in which people of every nation, tribe and language join the angels of heaven in praising God. Use these prayers from Revelation to join in that praise.

You are worthy to take the scroll
　and to open its seals,
because you were slain,
　and with your blood you purchased men for God
　from every tribe and language and people and nation.
You have made them to be a kingdom and priests to serve our
　　God,
　and they will reign on the earth . . .

Worthy is the Lamb, who was slain,
to receive power and wealth and wisdom and strength
and honor and glory and praise!
Revelation 5:9-10, 12

Salvation belongs to our God,
who sits on the throne,
and to the Lamb. . . .

Amen!
Praise and glory
and wisdom and thanks and honor
and power and strength
be to our God for ever and ever.
Amen!

Revelation 7:10, 12

JOURNAL
■ Responding to God

■ *Love to one another, says John, is the family likeness of God's children.*

Who among God's people has loved you? How did they show this? What difference has it made?

■ *God's love is an unselfish love. He loved us when there was nothing about us to move him to do anything other than blast and blight us for our ingrained irreligion—"he loved us and sent his Son to be the propitiation for our sins."*

How and to whom can you show the beginnings of this kind of love?

Thank God for his love.

19

Sons of God

■ **An Excerpt from** *Knowing God*

■ *What is a Christian? The question can be answered in many ways, but the richest answer I know is that a Christian is one who has God as his Father.*

But . . . sonship to God is not a universal status into which everyone enters by natural birth, but a supernatural gift which one receives through receiving Jesus. "No one comes to the Father"—in other words, is acknowledged by God as son—"except through me" (Jn 14:6).

Why might many religious people take offense at Jesus' statement?

How is Jesus' statement about the way to God different from what many people want to believe?

What does it mean to you that God (as you have come to know him through your study of this book) is your Father?

STUDY
■ Knowing the God of Scripture

Adoption into God's family begins here but lasts through eternity. Paul writes of the blessing of resurrection day that will make actual for us all that was implicit in the relationship of adoption, for it will introduce us into the full experience of the heavenly life now enjoyed by our older brother.

Read Romans 8:18-25. What do you see here that creates a sense of anticipation?

What connections do you see between God's people and God's natural creation?

Verse 21 speaks of being liberated from "bondage to decay and brought into the glorious freedom of the children of God." What do you think this will mean for other parts of God's creation? For you?

We are already children of God, yet verse 23 says that we "wait eagerly for our adoption as sons." Explain.

What do you particularly enjoy about being adopted by God?

REFLECT
■ Understanding the Character of God

■ *According to our Lord's own testimony in John's Gospel, God's fatherly relation to him implied four things.*

First, fatherhood implied authority. The Father commands and disposes; the initiative which he calls his Son to exercise is the initiative of resolute obedience to his Father's will. "I have come down from heaven not to do my will but to do the will of him who sent me"; "I have [completed] the work you gave me to do" (6:38; 17:4).

Second, fatherhood implied affection. "The Father loves the Son." "The Father hath loved me. . . . I have obeyed my Father's commands and remain in his love" (5:20; 15:9-10).

Third, fatherhood implied fellowship. "I am not alone, for my Father is with me." "The one who sent me is with me; he has not left me alone, for I always do what pleases him" (16:32; 8:29).

Fourth, fatherhood implied honor. God wills to exalt his Son. "Father . . . glorify your Son." "The Father . . . has entrusted all judgment to the Son, that all may honor the Son just as they honor the Father" (17:1; 5:22-23).

All this extends to God's adopted children. In, through and under Jesus Christ their Lord, they are ruled, loved, companied with and honored by their heavenly Father.

In your relationship with God your Father, how do you experience these four qualities?

authority:

affection:

fellowship:

honor:

PRAY

■ **Meeting God**

■ *Adoption is a family idea, conceived in terms of love, and viewing God as father. In adoption, God takes us into his family and fellowship—he establishes us as his children and heirs. Closeness, affection and generosity are at the heart of the relationship. To be right with God the Judge is a great thing, but to be loved and cared for by God the Father is a greater.*

Meditate on all that it means to be adopted by God; then compose a prayer of response.

■ *Were I asked to focus the New Testament message in three words, my proposal would be* adoption by propitiation, *and I do not expect ever to meet a richer or more pregnant summary of the gospel than that.*

JOURNAL
■ **Responding to God**

■ *The thought of our Maker becoming our perfect parent—
faithful in love and care, generous and thoughtful, interested
in all we do, respecting our individuality, skillful in training
us, wise in guidance, always available, helping us to find ourselves in maturity, integrity and uprightness—is a thought which can have
meaning for everybody, whether we come to it by saying, "I had a wonderful father, and I see that God is like that, only more so," or by saying, "My
father disappointed me here, and here, and here, but God, praise his name,
will be very different," or even by saying, "I have never known what it is to
have a father on earth, but thank God I now have one in heaven."*

Select one of the three statements above that is closest to your own
family experience and write your own response to God as your
Father.

■ *The depressions, randomness and immaturities that mark the children of
broken homes are known to us all. But things are not like that in God's family. There you have absolute stability and security; the parent is entirely
wise and good, and the child's position is permanently assured.*

20

THOU OUR GUIDE

READ
■ **An Excerpt from** *Knowing God*

■ *To many Christians, guidance is a chronic problem. Why? Not because they doubt that divine guidance is a fact, but because they are sure it is. They know that God can guide, and has promised to guide, every Christian believer. Books and friends and public speakers tell them how guidance has worked in the lives of others. Their fear, therefore, is not that no guidance should be available for them, but that they may miss the guidance which God provides through some fault of their own. When they sing*

> *Guide me, O thou great Jehovah,*
> *Pilgrim through this barren land;*
> *I am weak, but Thou art mighty,*
> *Hold me with Thy powerful hand:*
> *Bread of heaven,*
> *Feed me now and evermore*

they have no doubt that God is able both to lead and to feed, as they ask. But they remain anxious, because they are not certain of their own receptiveness to the guidance God offers.

What are some of your own questions about God's guidance?

STUDY
■ Knowing the God of Scripture

Read Psalm 25. What clues can you gain about the circumstances in which David wrote this psalm (vv. 1-3, 16-22)?

What kind of guidance would you expect a person to seek under these circumstances?

Note each word or phrase in the psalm that refers in some way to God's guidance. What does each contribute to an understanding of what it means to be guided by God?

What does this psalm reveal about God's nature?

What do you see here that addresses your own concerns about guidance?

Three times the psalmist declares, "My hope is in you" (vv. 3, 5, 21). What do you find in this psalm that brings you hope?

REFLECT
■ Understanding the Character of God

■ *The true way to honor the Holy Spirit as our guide is to honor the holy Scriptures through which he guides us. The fundamental guidance which God gives to shape our lives— the instilling, that is, of the basic convictions, attitudes, ideals and value judgments, in terms of which we are to live—is not a matter of inward promptings apart from the Word but of the pressure on our consciences of the portrayal of God's character and will in the Word. . . .*

"Be the kind of person that Jesus was"; "seek this virtue"; . . . "know your responsibilities—husbands, to your wives; wives, to your husbands; parents, to your children; all of you, to all your fellow Christians and all your fellow human beings; know them, and seek strength constantly to discharge them"—this is how God guides us through the Bible, as any student of the Psalms, the Proverbs, the Prophets, the Sermon on the Mount, and the ethical parts of the Epistles will soon discover. "Turn from evil and do good" (Ps 34:14; 37:27)—this is the highway along which the Bible is concerned to lead us, and all its admonitions are concerned to keep us on it. Be it noted that the reference to being "led by the Spirit" in Romans 8:14 relates not to inward "voices" or any such experience, but to mortifying known sin and not living after the flesh!

Only within the limits of this guidance does God prompt us inwardly in matters of "vocational" decision. So never expect to be aided to marry an unbeliever, or elope with a married person, as long as 1 Corinthians 7:39 and the seventh commandment stand! . . . The Spirit leads within the limits which the Word sets, not beyond them. "He guides me in paths of righteousness" (Ps 23:3)—but not anywhere else.

When has the Spirit spoken through Scripture to guide you away from sin and onto a path of righteousness?

PRAY
■ **Meeting God**

■ *Guidance, like all God's acts of blessing under the covenant of grace, is a sovereign act. Not merely does God will to guide us in the sense of showing us his way, that we may tread it; he wills also to guide us in the more fundamental sense of ensuring that, whatever happens, whatever mistakes we may make, we shall come safely home. Slippings and strayings there will be, no doubt, but the everlasting arms are beneath us; we shall be caught, rescued, restored. This is God's promise; this is how good he is.*

Bring to mind some of the troubling events of your life; then pray about them—in light of the kind of guidance described in the paragraph above.

■ *This is part of the wonder of God's gracious sovereignty. "I will repay you for the years the locusts have eaten" (Joel 2:25).*

JOURNAL
■ **Responding to God**

■ *Trouble should always be treated as a call to consider one's ways. But trouble is not necessarily a sign of being off track at all; for as the Bible declares in general that "many are the afflictions of the righteous" (Ps 34:19 KJV), so it teaches in particular that following God's guidance regularly leads to upsets and distresses which one would otherwise have escaped.*

When has the experience described above been true for you? Write about these events, your motives, the challenges to your faith, and any ultimate good (or harm) that came from that event.

■ *Sooner or later, God's guidance, which brings us out of darkness into light, will also bring us out of light into darkness. It is part of the way of the cross.*

21

THESE INWARD TRIALS

READ
- **An Excerpt from *Knowing God***

- *A certain type of ministry of the gospel is cruel. It does not mean to be, but it is. It means to magnify grace, but what it does is rather the opposite. . . . Isaiah once pictured the misery of inadequate resources in terms of short beds and narrow blankets (Is 28:20)—a sure recipe for long-term discomfort and discontent. . . .*

The type of ministry that is here in mind starts by stressing, in an evangelistic context, the difference that becoming a Christian will make. Not only will it bring us forgiveness of sins, peace of conscience and fellowship with God as our Father; it will also mean that, through the power of the indwelling Spirit, we will be able to overcome the sins that previously mastered us, and the light and leading that God will give us will enable us to find a way through problems of guidance, self-fulfillment, personal relationships, heart's desire and such like, which had hitherto defeated us completely. . . .

Our assertion is that, in order to appeal compellingly to human wistfulness, this type of ministry allows itself to promise at this point more than God has undertaken to perform in this world. . . . The preacher wants to win his hearers to Christ; therefore he glamorizes the Christian life, making it sound as happy and carefree as he can.

What is good about this kind of invitation to Christ?

What problems do you see?

STUDY
■ Knowing the God of Scripture

What do the passages below suggest about the function of hardship in the lives of God's people?

Job 23:10:

Isaiah 57:17-19:

Acts 14:21-22:

1 Corinthians 12:12-13:

Hebrews 12:5-11:

REFLECT

■ Understanding the Character of God

■ *What is grace? In the New Testament, grace means God's love in action toward people who merited the opposite of love. . . . What is the purpose of grace? Primarily, to restore our relationship with God. . . . How does God in grace prosecute this purpose? Not by shielding us from assault by the world, the flesh and the devil, nor by protecting us from burdensome and frustrating circumstances, nor yet by shielding us from troubles created by our own temperament and psychology; but rather by exposing us to all these things, so as to overwhelm us with a sense of our own inadequacy, and to drive us to cling to him more closely. This is the ultimate reason, from our standpoint, why God fills our lives with troubles and perplexities of one sort and another: it* is to ensure that we shall learn to hold him fast. *The reason why the Bible spends so much of its time reiterating that God is a strong rock, a firm defense, and a sure refuge and help for the weak, is that God spends so much of his time bringing home to us that we are weak, both mentally and morally, and dare not trust ourselves to find, or to follow, the right road.*

When we walk along a clear road feeling fine, and someone takes our arm to help us, as likely as not we shall impatiently shake him off; but when we are caught in rough country in the dark, with a storm getting up and our strength spent, and someone takes our arm to help us, we shall thankfully lean on him. And God wants us to feel that our way through life is rough and perplexing, so that we may learn thankfully to lean on him. Therefore he takes steps to drive us out of self-confidence to trust in himself—in the classical scriptural phrase for the secret of the godly life, to "wait on the Lord."

Pray
■ Meeting God

"Lord, why is this?" I trembling cried,
  "Wilt thou pursue Thy worm to death?"
"Tis in this way," the Lord replied,
  "I answer prayer for grace and faith.

"These inward trials I employ
  From self and pride to set thee free;
And break thy schemes of earthly joy,
  That thou may'st seek thy all in me."
John Newton

Talk to God about some of your own "inward trials." Seek grace and faith from him.

JOURNAL
■ Responding to God

■ *God can bring good out of the extremes of our own folly; God can restore the years that the locust has eaten. It is said that those who never make mistakes never make anything. . . . Through our mistakes, God teaches us to know his grace and to cleave to him in a way that would never happen otherwise. Is your trouble a sense of failure? the knowledge of having made some ghastly mistake? Go back to God; his restoring grace waits for you.*

We all make mistakes—some large, some small. In writing reflect on one of your mistakes. Invite God's grace and restoration.

22

THE ADEQUACY OF GOD

READ

■ **An Excerpt from** *Knowing God*

■ *Paul's letter to Rome is the high peak of Scripture, however you look at it. Luther called it "the clearest gospel of all." "If a man understands it," wrote Calvin, "he has a sure road opened to him to the understanding of the whole Scripture." Tyndale, in his preface to Romans, linked both thoughts, calling Romans "the principal and most excellent part of the New Testament, and most pure Euangelion, that is to say glad tidings and that we call gospel, and also a light and a way in unto the whole Scripture." All roads in the Bible lead to Romans, and all views afforded by the Bible are seen most clearly from Romans, and when the message of Romans gets into a person's heart there is no telling what may happen. . . . John Chrysostom had it read aloud to him once a week; you and I could do a lot worse than that.*

To what extent has the book of Romans permeated your life?

Take the next appropriate step regarding this important book.

STUDY
■ **Knowing the God of Scripture**

■ *As Romans is the high peak of the Bible, so chapter 8 is the high peak of Romans.*

Read Romans 8:31-39. What do you see here that points to the adequacy of God?

Focus on each of the questions in verses 31-35. What does each question invite you to think and to know about God?

Focus on verses 37-39. How do these verses help you to apprehend God's love?

If you were enduring a difficult time of life, what encouragement would you find here?

REFLECT
■ Understanding the Character of God

■ *The climax of our book has now been reached. We set out to see what it means to know God. We found that the God who is "there" for us to know is the God of the Bible, the God of Romans, the God revealed in Jesus, the Three-in-One of historic Christian teaching. We realized that knowing him starts with knowing about him, so we studied his revealed character and ways and came to know something of his goodness and severity, his wrath and his grace. As we did so, we learned to reevaluate ourselves as fallen creatures, not strong and self-sufficient as we once supposed, but weak, foolish and indeed bad, heading not for Utopia but for hell unless grace intervenes.*

Also, we saw that knowing God involves a personal relationship whereby you give yourself to God on the basis of his promise to give himself to you. Knowing God means asking his mercy and resting on his undertaking to forgive sinners for Jesus' sake.

Further, it means becoming a disciple of Jesus, the living Savior who is "there" today, calling the needy to himself as he did in Galilee in the days of his flesh. Knowing God, in other words, involves faith—assent, consent, commitment—and faith expresses itself in prayer and obedience. . . .

Now, finally, and on the basis of all that went before, we learn that a person who knows God will be more than conqueror, and will live in Romans 8, exulting with Paul in the adequacy of God. And here we have to stop, for this is as high in the knowledge of God as we can go this side of glory.

In your life, and as you contemplate needs in the world around you, what does it mean that God is entirely and gloriously adequate?

PRAY
■ Meeting God

"Thou hast said, 'Seek ye my face.' My heart says to thee, 'Thy face, LORD, do I seek.'" (Ps 27:8 RSV)

Write a prayer that expresses your own seeking after the face of God.

JOURNAL
■ Responding to God

■ *Once a person has truly given himself up to the Lord Jesus (so Paul is telling us), he never need feel the uncertainty of the cartoonist's lady who murmurs as she puffs at her thistledown, "He loves me—he loves me not." For it is the privilege of all Christians to know for certain that God loves us immutably, and that nothing can at any time part us from that love or come between us and the final enjoyment of its fruits.*

What are some of the forces that threaten your relationship with God? Acknowledge these threats in writing, and then respond within the strength of God's love.